Class
Dismissed!

Class Dismissed!

High School Poems
by Mel Glenn

Photographs by Michael J. Bernstein

Clarion Books
New York

For my parents—M.G.

The students in these poems are fictitious, and any
resemblance to actual persons is coincidental.

Clarion Books
a Houghton Mifflin Company imprint
215 Park Avenue South, New York, NY 10003
Text copyright © 1982 by Mel Glenn
Photographs copyright © 1982 by Michael J. Bernstein
All rights reserved.
For information about permission to reproduce
selections from this book, write to Permissions,
Houghton Mifflin Company, 2 Park Street, Boston, MA 02108
Printed in the USA

Library of Congress Cataloging in Publication Data

Glenn, Mel.
Class Dismissed! High school poems.
Summary: Original poems about the emotional lives
of contemporary high school students.
1. Children's poetry, American.
I. Bernstein, Michael J.   II. Title.
PS3557.L447M5   811'.54   81-38441
ISBN 0-89919-075-8   AACR2
PA ISBN 0-395-58111-7

HAL 10 9 8 7 6 5 4 3 2

Acknowledgments

My thanks to the many students I have taught through the years whose varied lives and personalities inspired the fictional students in these poems.   M.G.

My thanks to the real students who agreed to serve as models for the photographs in this book.   M.J.B.

Contents

Benjamin Heywood

School's all right if you don't take it seriously.
It's a good place, man, to meet females, give them
   the line.
I hang out and get high.
As long as I'm quiet in class, the teachers don't care.
No use botherin' each other.
Sometimes I give 'em a smile
To show I know they're tryin'.
Makes 'em feel good.
I even do a homework assignment now and then,
Just to keep my hand in.
I do the minimum.
I pass.
Nothin' important ever gets said.
If you want to disappear
Just sit in my math class for a bit.
I figure I'll be ready for college next year.

Marvin
Pickett

When I wear my football jersey to class
All the foxes give me the eye.
I am number one, the best there is.
Ain't nobody like me in the history of the school.
I am the greatest pass receiver in the world.
Last Saturday I faked two defenders out of their
    sneakers
And caught the touchdown that won the game.
School's for fillin' in the week, man.
On the football field I'm king.
Got it all figured out: two years J.C. ball,
Then college,
Then the draft,
Then the pros.
Hey, man, don't you believe me?
Ain't you listenin'?
I'm the best there is.

Rhonda
Winfrey

Senior year should be a breeze,
Easy courses and walks in the April rain.
But I've never been under so much pressure in my life.
I wake up every morning with knots in my stomach.
I have chewed my fingernails to my elbows
And those days without headaches are rare.
But even if my body totally deserts me,
It's a small price to pay for high grades and
        a good college.
I have to be the best.
Second place is no place at all.
Pass the Valium, please.
My mother warns me to slow down,
But I can't.
She doesn't know that life is a jungle,
Even in high school.

Eleanor Paine

When Rhonda read one of her poems in class
I sat there amazed
By a sensitivity I didn't know she possessed.
Isn't it enough for her just to be beautiful?
She talks to boys as easily as if they were
    her brothers.
She plays tennis as though she were training
    for Wimbledon.
She tells jokes like a professional comedienne.
A week later, while sitting in the dentist's office,
I saw her poem in a magazine.
Only it didn't have her name on it.
I don't understand.
Why when she has everything
Does she want even more?

Rickie
Miller

I come to school an hour before everyone else
And do my homework.
In the early morning light the school is as quiet
     as a church,
Blackboards clean,
Sun slanting in through the windows.
I quietly drink my coffee, eat my glazed doughnut.
My house, on the other hand, is a battle zone.
Arguments and accusations fly like rifle fire.
My mother and father threaten each other with divorce.
Neither has the guts to go through with it.
"You selfish bastard."
"You bitch."
"You don't make enough."
"This house is a mess."
I'm sick of standing in the crossfire.
One hour of peace isn't too much to ask for,
Is it?

Lisa Goodman

Nobody pays attention to me;
I'm average.
If I started to cut class,
Yell at the teacher,
Not do my homework,
Everybody would notice me.
But I don't do these things.
I never get into trouble.
Teachers don't call on me.
I'd like to think that one day
They will all stand up and see me,
But I don't think it will happen.
I once read in a play,
"Attention must be paid."
Not really.

Gordon Mathews

Yesterday I dragged myself to the library
To lose myself in the reference section.
I met a girl there;
(Me, of all people!
Me, who studies the wallpaper at parties,
Me, who stands near the phonograph, afraid to dance.)
We began to talk of wonderful things.
Poetry, for one,
Music, for another,
Hers and mine.
Her name is Lisa and her soft voice stirred me
To embroider stories I had long forgotten.
If I talked too much it was
Foolishness born from a desire
To be listened to with warm-eyed understanding.

Monica Zindell

When my mother found my birth control pills in my
    drawer
She threw me out of the house, calling me a tramp.
"You wanna play grown-up?" she screamed.
"Find out what it's like."
I left my home, hating her and promising myself
I would never return.
Now
    I cook,
      clean,
      wash,
      and, oh yeah, occasionally go to school.
    My boyfriend
      works late,
      drinks,
      stays out with his friends
      and, oh yeah, occasionally has time for me.
Life's a real blast.
I want to call up my mother and
Beg her to take me back.
I can't bring myself to pick up the phone.
Pride's a stubborn thing,
Especially when you're wrong.

Ellen Winters

Feeling closed in and cut off from life, I told my
Parents,
Who told me to tell my
Teacher,
Who referred me to my
Guidance counselor,
Who sent me to the
Assistant principal,
Who informed the
Principal,
Who said I should go back to my
Teacher,
Who told me to speak to my
Parents.

Robin Gold

Yesterday I received the news:
I didn't make the college of my first choice,
Nor of my second.
I feel so ashamed.
I didn't want anyone to see me cry.
But my teacher saw my face
And asked me what was wrong,
Before I could help it
The tears and the story came pouring out.
He tried to say the right words.
I could go to community college for a year
And then transfer over.
I know he meant well,
But I feel so bad, so stupid.
Is it possible for your life to fall apart at seventeen?
No doubt about it.

Nancy Soto

When my English teacher told me it was my turn to give a
    speech
I thought it was an invasion of privacy.
How could I explain that for me the spoken word
    says little?
I am the artist-in-residence in the castle of my dreams,
With rich portraits, my portraits, decorating the walls.
The sketches in my notebook breathe a purer air than I
    do.
Nervous and afraid, I brought my lords and ladies to
    class,
Hoping they would show what I could not tell.
I silently flipped the pages, saying nothing.
The class, waiting for me to speak, began to laugh.
I sat down, having said nothing, but exposing everything.

Ernest
Mott

When I was younger, mothers didn't let me play with
    their kids.
"Billy has to come in for supper."
A lie,
Because I could see the fear in their faces.
One time I did run naked through the neighborhood.
One time I did beat up this kid who called me "retard."
One time I did smash four windows in a row.
It wasn't my fault.
Something inside of me told me to do these things.
I was always sorry afterward.
Now, after years of special classes,
Years of Thorazine and therapy,
They want to put me back into a regular class.
I don't know if I want to go back,
Back to people who still have fear in their faces.

Danny Vargas

My father drinks, so I don't stay home much.
My teachers bore me, so I don't go to class much.
Baseball is my life,
My present and my future.
When I take the relay from Conti
And cut down the runner trying to score from first,
There's no thrill in the world that comes close,
Not even sex.
I have to scratch for everything,
Beating out grounders.
Dodging inside pitches.
Advancing the runner over to third.
I thought I was doin' fine
Until the coach threw me a nasty curve
That sent me sprawling to the dirt.
He said I couldn't play no more because
I had failed three subjects.
He asked me to turn in my uniform.
I refused and ran out of his office, crying,
Onto the field, to the batter's box,
To the only place I can call home.

Christopher Conti

My whole life is going great, no complaints.
One day I'll patrol the outfield in some
    major league park.
Right now I'm batting .405
And lead the club in RBIs.
The coach says I have real potential.
I finally found a girl I love;
Gracie is a real class lady,
(Though lately she's been acting kinda weird.)
I figure she and I will get married after high school.
She'll travel with me while I spend some time in
    the minors.
And then major leagues, here I come.
When I'm standing in center field,
There ain't no runner that can advance on me.
There ain't no catch I can't make.
There just ain't nothing that gets by me.

Grace DeLorenzo

I can't tell my father;
He would shoot me.
I can't tell my mother;
She would throw me out of the house.
I can't tell my sister;
She would rat on me.
I can't tell Chris;
He would offer to marry me,
For all the wrong reasons.
I'm so afraid and scared.
There's no one left to turn to.

Orlando Martinez

Did they find the guy who stabbed me?
All I know, I was hanging out in front of the school.
I pushed into this guy with my elbow.
He pushed back into me with a knife.
I was surprised to see a growing red circle on my shirt.
Then the pain started.
I ran into school and collapsed in the lobby.
Hands rushed at me to stop the fountain.
My life was saved at school.
Funny—all those days I spent cutting out,
Only to return blood-soaked and scared.
Did they ever find the guy who stabbed me?

David Eberhoff

Some people occasionally carry a camera.
I wear mine, everywhere, everyday.
I shudder to think where I'd be without one.
My Nikon is my passport to all the cliques
That would never accept me if I didn't
Record their faces for posterity.
Meetings, sports events, senior pictures—
I take them all, flattering all vanities.
Maria and I are a good team.
She writes the stories; I snap the pictures.
When the guy was stabbed in the school lobby
I caught the blood before horrified people shooed me
    away.
I wanted to run the shot in the school paper.
But the faculty adviser asked
How I could be so ghoulish.
I felt nothing, except what a wonderful picture it was.
It's not my fault that I can see the world only through
    a filter.

Christine Leader

Once, sitting in class, playing with the gold cross
    around my neck
I had a vision.
A shaft of light surrounded my paper.
I took it as a call to keep my mind and body pure.
I would devote my life to Christ
And bring His word to the unblessed.
The bell rang
And as I walked through the multitude to my next class
Some heathen ripped off my cross.
It's not so easy to find direction these days.

Thomas Kearns

You get good money for gold chains these days.
Ripped one off yesterday
Off this moony-looking girl.
Neat, man, I was halfway down the hall
Before she even turned around.
The trick is to get rid of the merchandise real quick.
Getting caught with it is a sucker's game.
I've been accused several times, even suspended.
But, man, they can't prove nothin'.
In a week I'm back,
Free to walk the halls,
Ready to strike again.

Franz Dominguez

I don't know whose fault it is.
There's enough blame to go around.
I always order a hamburger in a restaurant.
I can't read the menu.
I memorize the number of stops on the train.
I can't read the signs.
I know TV cartoons by heart.
TV Guide is much too hard for me.
I think I could learn to read if someone sat with me,
But teachers don't seem to have the time.
Words fly right by me.
Sometimes, when no one's around, I punch the wall.
I'm frightened by my own anger.

Catherine Heath

"He looked at her with eyes full of passion."
"He longed to bestow a thousand kisses on her sinuous
    neck."
"He wanted to carry her off to his castle in the north
    country."
The Victorian novel of my daydream is interrupted
By Allen poking me for my homework.
Why are the boys in this school such babies, not
    noblemen?
I'd like to be relieved of my virginity.
My gift to an especially deserving young swain.
Only, there are no men hanging round the manor,
Just boys hiding behind their acne.
Life doesn't imitate art,
But at least it should make the attempt
To prove that romance is still possible in a graceless
    world.

Allen Greshner.

"Hello."

> Pause, skin tight, small planet orbiting the sun,
> flash of her smile, freckle, worried she'll say
> yes, worried she'll say no,

"Tracy, This is Allen."

> Lovely name, I'll marry her, stomach tight, voice
> cracking, do it already, don't hang up, get to the
> point, pause,

"Would you like to go to the prom with me?"

> Guillotine blade, pause, hates me, fill the space,
> no is better than no sound, small hope, sinking,

"Can't make it?"

> Why, what's wrong, what's wrong with me, big feet,
> who else can I ask, hate proms, sweaty tux, sounded
> too young, stomach churning,

"I understand."

> No, I don't, don't choke, be cool, sound mature,
> black hole in the universe, nothing ever goes right
> for me, alone, relieved,

"Good night."

Maria Preosi

I was always known as "Tracy's sister,"
Even by my friends.
In the unspoken competition between us
I was always judged by her blond hair and giggly laugh.
I lost the race at the starting line.
For years I sat at her desk, two years behind,
Plotting.
Anger churned within me, an oil-black rage.
I wanted to kill for every injustice ever done to me.
Yet I accepted calmly, meekly,
My position in her shadow
And did not even whisper a syllable of revenge.

Eric
Theodore

The grass is always greener on the next date, I think
And I judge my manliness on how many I can make
    for the week.
Three is the average:
Friday night, Saturday night, and for the new girl,
Sunday afternoon.
As one girl fades another takes her place
In my little black book.
Scoring is what it's all about.
Even if I strike out with one, my batting average is
    still high.
Last Saturday I went out dancing with Julie.
I felt nothing for her, not really.
Our laughing was empty,
Our dancing mechanical.
"I had a good time," she said afterward.
"So did I," I lied.
I'll probably take her out again next week.

Julie
Snow

All week long I sit in class counting the hours
    to the weekend.
And when Friday finally comes, I dance the night away.
The music blasts; my body rocks.
It doesn't matter which guy takes me dancing.
I just use them for the price of admission.
My real boyfriend is away at college.
But when he's not around, I go out all the time,
With all sorts of guys,
And give them just enough to keep them interested.
Sometimes, when I'm alone, I worry about my
    reputation,
But when the music starts, I forget everything.

Jason Talmadge

I picked a fight with my soon-to-be-stepfather
To see whose side my mother would take.
Silly of me, because I already knew the answer.
"Jason," my mother said, "why are you acting like this?
Max likes you."
The hell he does.
He would like nothing better than to have
My mother all to himself.
I took two buses over to my father's apartment
To ask whether I could live with him.
Silly of me, because I already knew the answer.
"I'd love to have you here, Jason," he said,
"But you know how it is.
The judge said you had to live with your mother.
Besides, the apartment is too small;
You know I tried, kid."
The hell he did.
They both want a life of their own,
A life which doesn't include me.
If I am such a burden to both of them,
Why did they have me in the first place?

Dora Antonopolis

I know you are not happy with me, Poppa.
You want me to be the little girl
Who stays home and waits on you hand and foot.
I know you have my whole life planned out.
You smother me with hard smiles
Which reflect no warmth but your grim determination
To keep me tied to you.
(And here I thought only mothers had umbilical cords.)
Do you know, Poppa, I read romantic novels
Which place me a million miles away from you?
Do you know I work after school
To earn the money you never give me?
Do you know I secretly meet young men
Just to hurt you?
Do you know I have a heart? A mind?
I doubt it, Poppa.
I want to be a doctor.
I want to be a surgeon, Poppa,
And sever forever the ties that bind us.

Norman Moskowitz

My grandfather's picture sits on my desk
While I do my homework.
My father spent money on me.
My grandfather spent time.
As I struggle with trig and other responsibilities
I remember how my grandfather would
Take me for walks in the park,
Explain how a screwball was thrown,
Encourage me to think well of myself.
I really don't want to wrestle with world history,
The gross national product and Nathaniel Hawthorne.
I just want to go to the park with you again, Grandpa.

Marie Yeagerman

My mother saw my report card
And said, "Don't worry, you'll do better next time."
My father saw my college bulletins
And said, "Don't worry, there'll always be money for
    you."
My sister saw me exercising
And said, "Don't worry, you'll lose weight."
I just wish people would stop killing me with kindness
And just tell me the God-honest truth:
I'm dumb.
I'm poor.
I'm fat.
Then maybe I could face a realistic world
And begin to repair the damage.

Jeanette
Jaffe

I told my friend Marie that I loved our French teacher,
    Mr. Kensington.
She said he's married.
I said I didn't mind.
I can't sit in his class
Without all kinds of fantasies
Going through my mind.
One day I had to leave his room.
He asked me if I was all right.
He should only know.
Last week I put a letter in his mailbox,
Saying on paper what I was afraid to say in person.
Only I didn't sign my name—this time.
But just you wait, Mr. Kensington.
You're in for a big surprise.

Jill
Le Claire

Everyone is trying to raise my consciousness.
My friend Amy says I must work on the Third World
    relief committee.
My mother drags me to meetings of NOW.
My brother wants me to picket the UN.
My father quizzes me from *Time* magazine,
And my boyfriend composes no-nuke protest songs.
I just want to be a cheerleader.
I just love the white sweater and blue pom-poms.
Amy says I'm politically naive.
My mother clucks her tongue in disapproval.
My brother refuses to introduce me to his friends.
My father just goes on reading his newspaper,
And my boyfriend goes to rallies alone.
I just want to be a cheerleader
And scream myself hoarse when our team scores.

Jodi Kurtz

When my sister, Debbie, went away to college
I was thrilled because I got her room.
She told me what teachers to take in high school,
What books to read.
I have always followed in her footsteps.
Now I don't know.
She has come home from college in mid-semester
Nervous and exhausted, needing a break she says.
I hate the pauses between my questions and her answers.
I am sitting in the library
Trying to dream up a topic for my *Hamlet* term paper.
My thoughts swim in slow circles.
I see the skeleton in my closet holding an extra hanger.
I'd like to know if it's my turn to step inside.

Brenda Stewart

Jill is so straight, I can't stand it.
But I need a friend who helps me touch the ground
While I chase the wind.
If I am a high-flying kite,
Jill is my string.
If I want to buy something outrageous,
She reminds me that it's not machine washable.
If I act like a complete idiot,
She tells me there is still hope.
If I have a fight with my parents,
She reminds me that it will soon blow over.
Last Saturday I wanted to go shopping with her,
But she had a game to cheer.
I went to the mall myself and
Walked through the aisles admiring everything.
Without thinking, I pulled a top off one of the shelves
And stuffed it into my bag.
A hand grabbed my arm.
A face asked me questions.
A finger dialed a phone.
I felt so embarrassed.
I kept thinking I wouldn't be in this mess
If Jill had come shopping with me.

Rosemarie Stewart

Responsible,
Trustworthy,
Kind,
Quiet,
Obedient,
A girl scout without the uniform.
You would think all that is enough to win
My parents' love.
But in the theater of our house
Brenda holds center stage. She is
Irresponsible,
Sneaky,
Mean,
Loud,
Rebellious.
Her negative traits far outweigh the 100s I bring home.
When the cops called I felt sad,
Not for the trouble she was in,
But for the fact that once again
She cast herself in the starring role.

Hildy
Ross

"How did you get that nasty bruise on your
    cheek, Hildy?"
"Fell off my bike, Mr. Gray. Ten speeds are
Tricky to get used to at first."
I sure as hell was not going to tell him my father
    hit me again.
Actually, it's been a pretty good year,
Only been beat up four times,
Once for coming home late,
Once for talking back,
Once for a poor report card,
And once for no reason at all.
My boyfriend offered to punch my father
    out for me.
But that would get me in even more trouble.
I try to stay out of my father's way,
Which works most of the time.
Yeah, I know there are agencies for this sort of thing,
But I can't see turning him in.
He's still my father.

Peter Quincy

Lacking an imagination of my own, I rely on Billy's.
Lacking any confidence in my own abilities, I rely
    on his.
He is the tall tree in whose shade I feel protected.
We first met in a schoolyard basketball game four
    years ago.
"I'll take the runt," he said.
But he said it so nicely it was impossible to take
    offense.
I hang around him all the time, like a kid brother,
Jealous if anyone else gets too close.
So what if I play tortoise to his hare?
He still includes me in his race.
He can make anyone laugh—teachers, parents, friends—
While I mope a lot and let little things bother me.
One day I am sure he will drop me.
But until then I will cling to him,
Happy that he has included me in one more game.

Billy
Paris

This term I don't have a lunch period,
Too many subjects to make up.
So while I learn new nouns in Mr. Brewer's Spanish class,
I munch on some potato chips.
Two days ago he laid down the law:
"No snacking while speaking Spanish."
Yesterday I got even.
I pulled out from my bag
A checkered tablecloth,
Two candlesticks,
One bowl,
One spoon,
And a thermos full of soup.
I slowly set the table,
Said a blessing (in Spanish) over the food,
And named every object with perfect accent.
Mr. Brewer stood there, dumbstruck.
Then he began to laugh.
The class joined in.
You know, school doesn't have to be so grim.

Lauren Jones

I hate the way I look.
I have been put together in pieces from different puzzles.
My eyes are so weak my glasses are on loan from
    an observatory.
My nose is so big I can join the circus as a clown.
My breasts are so small I can wear my brother's
    undershirt.
If my body is supposed to be my temple
I'd like to change religions right now.
I guess when I'm older and can afford it
I can get everything fixed—
My eyes, my nose, my breasts.
But what am I supposed to do in the meantime?
I remember a proverb I read once:
"To know beauty, one must live with it."
To know ugliness, one must live with that, too.

Sheila Franklin

Shari and I have known each other since the fourth
     grade.
She lived in my house and I lived in hers
To the point where people thought we were sisters.
She led; I followed.
She told me what clothes to wear, what lipstick to use.
I loved her because when people hurt me
She defended me.
If someone said I had the personality of a rock,
She said I was just shy.
If someone said I was basically ugly,
She said I would be truly exotic one day.
Friends are forever, or so I thought.
When she discovered boys, I discovered
That the time between phone calls lengthened.
I see her once in a while,
A quick hello in the halls.
I remember the times we rode our bikes together
All day long in the hot summer sun.

Shari Morrow

My mother hassled me about boys,
Always.
If I went out with one exclusively, she said
I was tying myself down.
If I dated many, she said
I should be more selective.
She waited up for me on Saturday night,
Wanting to hear all the details.
In a burst of independence
I told her to mind her own business.
I told her I wanted a life of my own.
I threatened to move out—to Grandma's house.
So now when I turn the key at two A.M.
I still half expect to see her in her bathrobe.
Guess she's lost interest in me.

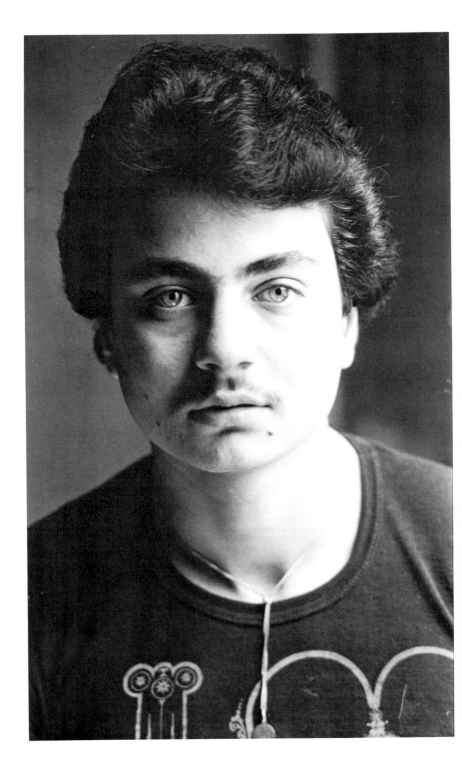

Michael
Ravenall

I don't know why you won't give me the car keys, Dad.
Are you afraid I'll drink while I drive?
Are you afraid I'll total the car like Steven did?
Are you afraid I'm still too young?
Or too old?
What's the matter, Dad?
I went to driving school.
I passed my road test on the first try.
I can take apart an engine in my sleep.
I marked soup cans in the A & P for a year to pay for
    the insurance.
Are you so afraid I'll drive out of your life forever?
Don't worry, Dad. You're okay.
Even though I haven't told you that in years.

Sanford Evans Pierce

When most students didn't know the Midwest from the
    Mid-East,
When most students thought Parliament was a cigarette,
I watched the news, studied the campaigns, and took
    notes.
I did an analysis of each candidate's position on the
    issues.
I rang doorbells, once for the Democrats,
Once for the Republicans.
My friends asked me why I got so excited by politics.
I replied that I cared what happened.
Our country faces great challenges in the years ahead, I
    explained.
I contemplated what changes I could make as president
Of the Student Council.
And waged a campaign that was both thoughtful and
    high-minded.
In our school debate I spoke passionately of the
Beauty of public service and the goodness of all men.
My audience went to sleep.
Sensing defeat, I promised music in the cafeteria.
I won.
One must be sensitive to the needs of his constituents.

Alison
Ford

The boys I meet want just one thing only.
They stare at my breasts as if they were some
Promised ticket to paradise.
I know I'm not ready for a sexual relationship.
I don't know if I'm ready for a relationship, period.
But I think it would be nice to have
Someone to hold me,
Someone who would make me laugh,
Someone who would see more than my body.
Last year, on a trip with my family, I met a guy
    from Maine.
We talked, just talked the whole night
And I never felt closer to anyone in my life.
In the morning he had to leave in his van
And I went back to school,
Fending off the boys who want just one thing only.

Raymond
Crystal

It seems to me that school sails along like a ship
With watertight compartments separating knowledge.
A compartment for math,
One for history
And so on right down the length of the ship.
Order is fine, I suppose
But my brain doesn't come in grapefruit sections.
And while my lab partner happily whistles
When he cuts up our frog,
I'm thinking about sex.
I think about sex mostly all the time,
Especially with Alison.
When the outside me is writing up my lab report
The inside me is thinking of a half-dozen ways
I can get that beautiful girl.
The bell rings and that magnificent vessel, Alison,
Glides out the door.
On the school ship they have a law against sex
And dreaming.

Carrie
Pearson

The first time I had sex with Raymond
It hurt so much I yelled at him to stop,
But he didn't hear me.
He was someplace else, pushing again and again;
And when he finally broke through,
Collapsing like a punctured balloon,
He shouted out another girl's name.
Raymond, how could you!
He apologized with kisses and promises.
I said it's forgotten.
Now when we do it, it's easier,
Even fun.
But I'll never really forgive him.
Never.

Donna Vasquez

My friend Anna tells me to stay in school,
But I don't see how I'm gonna make it.
I tried, man, but it's no good.
Maybe I can't be smart with the books.
¿Qué va?—What does it matter?
All that readin' just wastes my time
When I can be out makin' money.
I love fixin' people's hair,
The way it is in fashion magazines.
I work part-time and my boss is proud of me.
Anna tells me to stick it out,
That I only have a little ways to go.
But it's no good.
When I'm in school they make me feel like a child.
("Do that again and you'll get another zero.")
When I'm working,
When I'm out in the real world,
I feel like a woman.
Lo siento—I'm sorry, Anna; it's no good.
I'll do your hair for graduation.

Anna
Montalvo

When I was a baby you sang me soft Spanish lullabies.
The moon above San Juan looked as large as a
    grapefruit.
Then we came here and all the music stopped.
You want me to spend my life sewing dresses?
You want me to get a job at the five-and-ten?
No, Momma, I want so much more.
I'm twenty and still in high school
But I'm gonna graduate, I swear it.
I don't know how, but I'm gonna do it.
I know I failed English three times.
I know I hung out on the streets for a year.
But I know I'm gonna graduate, I swear it.

Susan Tulchin

It started in kindergarten when the teacher
Reported to my parents in tones usually reserved
    for funerals
That I kept to myself,
Reversed letters,
Answered questions that weren't asked.
And while my friends paraded their reading abilities
    like new dresses,
I struggled to make sense of the circles and lines.
My parents, fearing the label "learning disability"
More than "just plain dumb,"
Said nothing to the school,
But privately took me to a clinic
Where each week I battled through the clouds.
When I failed a test in school, I cried,
Not for myself, but for the pain my parents didn't show.
"Ssh, baby, it's all right," they would say.
But it's not.
I hear them arguing far into the night.

Laurie Allen

To all those who warned me against dangers I was
    afraid to risk,
To my girl friend who said boys just take advantage,
To my father who lectured me about riding in cars,
To my mother who cautioned me about dancing close,
To all those love letters I thought of but never wrote,
To all the no sayers, balloon deflators, dream robbers,
Screw you all!
Kevin kissed me.

Kevin McDonald

I thought I would be a sports announcer
Until my speech teacher told me I couldn't because
    I had a lisp.
I thought I would be a doctor
Until a bloody frog in biology convinced me otherwise.
I thought I would be a pilot
Until I got airsick on the shuttle to Boston.
All my plans for the future seem to dissolve in midair.
Am I depressed?
No way!
Laurie loves me.

Dominique Blanco

These are supposed to be the best years of my life;
They aren't.
Friends are supposed to be faithful;
They're not.
Teachers are supposed to know how to teach;
They don't.
I have spent four years here on the edge of everything—
Friends, parties, classes—
Rejecting myself before others had a chance to do it.
I cannot remember one good time I've had here.
When the yearbook came out, I complained to the
        adviser.
They left out my picture.
It figures.

Annie
Scarella

My mother worries about my social life these days.
I worry about my social life these days.
I don't have any.
"Why don't you have any fun?" she says. "I did
When I was your age."
My mother should only know what fun consists of
    these days:
Getting bombed,
Getting stoned,
Getting laid.
It's so hard to be decent anymore,
So hard to find friends that are normal.
So all I do on weekends is baby-sit.
And while my bank account grows larger,
My love life takes a back seat to
Running noses and Dr. Seuss stories.
My mother taught me to be a good girl.
Whatever for?

Mitchell Chapin

I can still see my father sitting in front of the TV,
Not saying a word, his eyes fixed on Walter Cronkite.
He looks old in his red robe.
If I wanted to speak, a wave of his hand silenced me.
I watched with him, bookends on the oppposite ends
    of the sofa,
Substituting nearness for closeness.
He was always formal with me, like I was a guest.
And when he died the silences in the house just
    continued.
Last week, while hunting for a pair of sneakers in
    a closet,
I discovered a manila folder filled with his poems.
Sad, lovely, lonely poems about nature, religion,
    and our family.
There were several poems about me,
Expressing a love I never knew nor felt.
Oh, Daddy, why didn't you read them to me when
    it mattered?
Didn't you think me more important than the evening
    news?

Charlie Wallinsky

I have a history teacher so old that
When she talks about the Civil War
It's from personal experience.
Her notes are so old
I think they were written on stone tablets.
She never looks up from them.
The printed word protects her from her pupils.
I decided to create a student—Altin Egors.
If there was homework I handed in two assignments.
If there was an examination I handed in two papers.
One day I thought the jig was up.
She peered over her notes and asked for Altin Egors.
I said quickly he had just left;
He wasn't feeling well.
She said, "Tell him his paper on witchcraft was superb."
I said, "Sure thing."
She went back to her notes, never to emerge again.
I sat back in my seat, smiling like the Cheshire cat.

Amy
Pines

Let my girl friend wear designer jeans.
Let my sister perm her hair.
Chic clothes and fancy sets may become some girls,
But they don't do a thing for me.
(I'm really quite plain-looking, so I have been told.)
My teacher teases me when I wear my plaid shirt
    and bib overalls.
Who does he want me to dress like—Vickie Vassar?
No, man, that ain't my style.
Yet sometimes I feel I'm locked into my look.
I yearn to play Cinderella.
Once, on a bet, I actually put on a skirt.
Someone in class yelled out, "Hey, man, who died?"
Nobody.
Nobody except my formal self.

Carl Immerman

Ever try to kiss a girl through a wire fence?
It can't be done.
But now girls, line up.
I'm gonna make up for lost time.
I want to scream it to the world,
Yell it from the mountain tops.
Today is the happiest day of my life.
Rickie, my friend,
Why are you sitting in that classroom alone?
Come out and hear my good news.
Today I am liberated,
Free at last, free at last,
Great God I'm free at last.
Today I will laugh and not just smile.
Today I will gorge myself on seven eclairs.
Today I will join the human race.
My braces finally came off!

Gail
Larkin

Dialogue of the unspoken argument:

Me: I want to go out of town to school.
       I want to get away from this crazy house.
       I want to leave my so-called friends
       And find really good ones.
       I want to find a boy who will love
       My wit, my intelligence and sense of humor,
       And my body.
       I want to run; I want to explore
       A world not defined by you.
       I want to go out of town to school.

Them: We want you to stay in the city for school.
       We want you to keep feeling the loving security
           of our home.
       We want you to stay with your friends because
       Who knows what creeps you'll find out there.
       Eventually, we want you to find a boy
       Who will appreciate you like we do, settle down
       And raise a family.
       We want you here, safe, because
       You are an extension of ourselves and our love.
       We want you to stay in the city for school.

Dialogue of the spoken argument:

"Honey, we'd love to send you out of town, but we can't
Afford to. You understand."
"Yeah, I understand. It's OK."

81

Joy McNair

The teachers think I'm sick
Because I always have my head down on the desk.
I'm ashamed to tell them I'm just tired,
So tired I can hardly keep my eyes open.
My father skipped town when I was nine.
My mother takes care of my two-year-old.
And I work a full shift at McDonald's,
At night.
I'm not complaining, not that it would do much good.
But it's hard to juggle my three lives.
My adolescence was stolen from me
By promises made and then broken.
I was in such a hurry to experience life all at once.
Now I'm paying the price,
In hamburgers.

Faith
Plotkin

I cut out a lot because school's a gigantic bore.
Want to test me on the movies I've seen?
Sorry, I do not know
Who directed what film in which year,
Who did the lighting,
Who did the casting.
It didn't matter who was playing,
Zorro, Zeppo, Tweetie-Bird, or Redford.
It didn't matter that I was alone,
Unbothered,
Unthinking,
Unworried
About where my life was to go.
Popcorn is a fine friend for those
Who don't wish to see the harsh light of day.
Can I please stay in the movies forever?

Adam Whitney

My father teaches in a nearby junior high.
Every night he works on his lessons.
He really cares what happens to his students.
His desk is a mess and he can't balance his checkbook.
He talks about moral right and wrong
And the Kennedy assassinations.
He's hopelessly out of date.
He tells me I should read the great philosophers and
    novelists,
(Never mind the Mickey Mouse work they give you in
    high school.)
He really believes that money can't buy happiness
And spends whatever he has taking the family on trips to
    old battlefields.
He's hopelessly out of date.
I tell him his values are old-fashioned.
He says I've already sold out to the Establishment.
He's hopelessly out of date.
Yet, one day,
When I'm a father and have kids of my own,
I hope I can be so hopeless.

Pamela Atkinson

I drink like a fish, you know,
Really no more than most of my friends.
Ssh—don't tell anyone.
My father would kill me if he found out.
He calls me his "princess."
He has placed me on a pedestal so high
My feet haven't touched the ground in years.
Monday through Friday I live in his fairy-castle world,
Do my work and never talk back,
Kiss him on the cheek when he comes home.
But on the weekend the princess gets polluted,
One drink, two drinks,
Three drinks, a few drinks.
Ssh—I don't want to say too much more;
I'll incriminate myself.
I think I'll take the fifth.

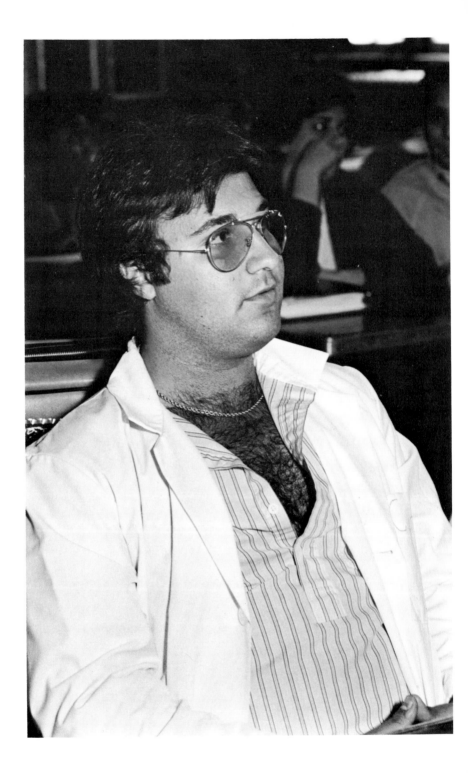

Joel
Feit

It takes talent to fail gym three times.
It's my protest against the body beautiful.
I can't jump the side horse or climb the ropes.
Running bores me and basketball is the pits.
I can't touch my toes or do a decent sit-up.
A jumping jack looks ridiculous and parallel bars
        are lethal.
The gym teacher says I'm not thinking positively.
I suppose I'm not.
But what's so great about smelly bodies and wet towels?
Everyone is so into their bodies these days.
Everyone is running far ahead of me,
Jumping higher,
Scoring points,
Breaking records.
I'd rather sit here and solve equations in my head.
As long as my mind is in good shape,
I don't much care about the rest of me.

Bernard Pearlman

(Thoughts in a math class)

Help!
I'm being eaten by a parabola.
He sees me as his arc enemy.
Radii, chords, and diameters are out to bisect me.
Help!
He's munching on me
Like a piece of π.
I tried to talk to him in his own language,
Parables.
No dice.
My chances of success are one in six,
Probably.

Song
Vu Chin

I have seen mothers cradling dead babies in their arms,
Afraid to let go, afraid not to.
I have seen children with bloated bellies cry,
With no strength left to make sounds.
I have seen open wounds so large
A man's fist could fit inside.
I have seen people eat dead dogs on the highway.
I have run with my family to flee these pictures of death,
But at night
The nightmares remind me I have not run far enough.
In this new country my body grows.
But at school I look into the faces around me,
Wide-eyed, well-fed, unblinking.
How could they know?
How could they not know?
America, Land of the Free, Home of the Ignorant.

Saul Steiner

I know it's not fashionable to admit I like reading
When others, like Michelle, are Mork-minded soap opera
    slaves.
If they stare at test patterns, I'll read *Tess*.
If they disco, I'll read Dante.
For there exists an elegance to the printed page
That can't be matched by a panty-hose commercial.
I really enjoy writing term papers,
Like the one I did on Machiavelli for world history.
Libraries protect me, making me feel like an intellectual
Miniver Cheevy.
I do wonder, though, if the grass is greener in
    an illiterate country,
As I spend Saturday night reading Sartre.
My books cannot completely camouflage other increasing
    desires.
I wake up in the night, wet and exhausted.
In literature they call this "mind versus heart."
I don't have the everyday vocabulary to explain it
    to myself.

Stella
Kolsky

Last week my brother jumped from the roof of our
    apartment house
And in the process killed a whole family.
He was always selfish, thinking the world revolved
    around him,
Which it did.
My father promptly had a stroke.
He babbles in the hospital about bicycles and
    teddy bears.
My mother, afraid to go out, walks on tiptoes
    from room to room.
And I feel cheated.
In school I sit staring at the walls;
I can't eat.
I can get through the day without speaking to anyone,
Running out the string of my own life.
It's as if he had taken my hand when he jumped.
Martin, what were you thinking on the way down?

Darcy Tanner

When I told my mother she didn't look well,
Could I get her something, she said,
"Stop stalling and practice your piano."
I told her I wanted to go out and play baseball.
"Nonsense," she said, "girls don't play baseball,
They play sonatas."
When I told my mother she'd get well soon,
Did she want her pills, she said,
"Stop stalling and practice your piano."
I told her there was nothing cheerful I could play.
"Nonsense," she said, "Look in your collection and
      find something."
When my mother died
I stopped stalling and practiced my piano.
I spend my time now going through my collection
And playing those minor chords over and over again.

Helen Price

Valedictory Speech: Second Draft (presented)

Parents, friends, teachers: On this special day
We are gathered here to celebrate, not an end,
But a beginning.
I will never forget the friends that I've made,
The knowledge I've gained, the fun I've had.
The world is beset by many problems,
But if we all work together, hand in hand,
The future holds a limitless bounty.
I want to thank my parents for inspiring me.
I want to thank my teachers for their time and devotion.
I want to thank . . .

Valedictory Speech: First Draft (crumpled in wastebasket)

Parents, friends, teachers: On this ordinary day
We are gathered here to ridicule the end of four
    insane years.
I will never forget the friends who knifed me in the
    back for grades,
The asinine facts I had to memorize, the misery I
    endured.
The world is beset by many problems; I really don't care.
It's impossible for human beings to get along with
    each other
And I'm seriously worried that the world will blow
    itself up.
I want to thank my parents for nagging me to death.
I want to thank my teachers for nothing.
I want to throw up. . . .

93

Donald Kaminsky

Put a heading on your paper like this.
Sit in a particular seat.
Ask the teacher for a room pass.
Memorize these words.
Eat lunch at a certain time.
How could I learn to make decisions for myself,
    I thought,
When every decision is made for me?
Wash your hands before dinner.
Pick up your socks.
Walk the dog.
Take out the garbage.
How could I learn to order my life, I thought,
When every order is given to me?
All my life I have been the last link in the
Chain of commands that never stopped.
Seeking to please everybody,
Needing the approval of all,
I followed all the orders, all the commands.
One night, slightly drunk, I decided on my own to get
A tattoo,
Actually two,
A $35 panther on one arm,
A $75 rose, (inscribed "Mother") on the other.
A man has to stand up for himself.
Hey, Ma, do you like them?

Stuart Rieger

Inscriptions in my yearbook:
"Best Wishes," (eight of them).
"Good Luck," (six of them).
"Keep in Touch," (four of them).
"Have a Nice Life," (two of them).
Wonderful!
Surely, four years could have produced more,
A little more feeling, a lot more warmth.
But the fault is mine, fellow graduates.
When you went to football games, parties, and dances,
I stayed home and studied my brains out,
Always worried that this quiz or that test
Would irrevocably determine my future.
I made my choice to live in the future tense
And forfeited all happiness in the present one.
So, forgive me if I just sign your book, "Best Wishes."
It's the best I can do under the circumstances.